Procedures Relating to a Federal Lapse in Appropriations

Table of Contents

I.   Requirements and Limitations

During a federal funding hiatus, or lapse in appropriations, the Department of Homeland Security (DHS) must be able to cease its government operations in an orderly fashion. Only those functions and activities that are exempt from the work restrictions specified in the Anti-Deficiency Act (ADA) may continue during a lapse in appropriations.

The ADA codifies the Constitutional requirement that "No Money shall be drawn from the Treasury, but in consequence of appropriations made by Law." Federal officials are prohibited from entering into contracts, incurring obligations, or performing activities without having a current appropriation, unless authorized by law. The Act further restricts acceptance of voluntary services or personal services beyond authorized levels "except for emergencies involving the safety of human life or the protection of property." As a result, only activities that qualify as exempt may continue to operate during a lapse in appropriations.

In accordance with Section 124 of Office of Management and Budget (OMB)'s 2014 Circular A-11, "Agency Operations in the Absence of Appropriations," the Department has developed the procedures outlined in this document as its contingency plan. Included, and as also specified by the A-11 guidance, is the identification of the following information:

1. An estimate, to the nearest half-day, of the time necessary to accomplish an orderly closure.
2. The total number of DHS employees on-board before implementation of the plan.
3. The total number of employees expected to be exempt from a lapse in appropriations.

Upon notification from OMB and subsequent direction from the DHS Under Secretary for Management (USM), DHS Components must adhere to the guidelines as set forth in the following pages. This includes the preparation of employee notices of furlough, the processing of personnel and pay records in connection with furlough actions, and the release of employees subject to a furlough in accordance with applicable law and regulations of the Office of Personnel Management (OPM).

Failure to maintain and adhere to these procedures may result in a violation of the ADA.

II. Definitions; Determining Exempt Functions and Employees

A. Definitions

The Department uses the term "exempt" to describe functions and employees who may be required to continue to perform during a federal funding hiatus. Other agencies in the Federal Government use different terminologies, including "excepted" and "essential." To avoid confusion from using multiple terms, guidance in this document will use the single term of "exempt" to refer to any employee who will continue working during a lapse in appropriations and who is not subject to a furlough during a funding hiatus.

Additionally, either an "emergency furlough" or a "federal funding hiatus" may be used to refer to a lapse in appropriations during which employees may be exempt.

B. Exempt Functions

Guidelines for exempt activities follow. Proposals to continue activities that do not fit in the guidelines should be directed immediately to the DHS Office of General Counsel (OGC).

The following activities and/or functions may continue during a lapse of appropriations:

1. Funded by Sources Other than Annual Appropriated Funds.

   Some functions are covered by fee revenues or by multi-year, no-year, or revolving funds (when the revolving fund has not lapsed), or advance appropriations, and if those accounts have sufficient carry-over balance, they would not be affected by a lapse of annual appropriations. Agencies may continue to incur obligations and disburse funds from such non-lapsed funding sources. Revolving funds that operate almost entirely on offsetting collections from other federal entities may also be forced to close, unless sufficient retained earnings are available to forestall the closure. Employees paid directly from a funding source that has not lapsed during a lapse in appropriations will continue to perform normal duties and will continue to receive pay during the lapse.

   > **EXAMPLES:**
   >
   > - The Disaster Relief Fund, which is funded by a no-year appropriation and may have sufficient balances available to continue operations
   > - Fee-funded activities such as those performed by U.S. Citizenship and Immigration Services

Of note, the DHS Working Capital Fund (WCF) requires authorization through the yearly appropriations act to continue operations, and thus, activities funded through the WCF must cease in the event of a lapse.

2. Authorized under Law to Continue Even without Funding.

Pursuant to a determination by the U.S. Department of Justice (DOJ), functions authorized by law to proceed during an appropriations lapse include "those functions as to which express statutory authority to incur obligations in advance of appropriations has been granted."

Active duty military members are exempt because their entitlement to pay is provided under 37 U.S.C. § 204. This entitlement means that DHS is authorized by law to incur obligations for their pay. These active duty service members may perform normal duties during a lapse.

In addition, Congress provides express authority for some agencies to enter into contracts or to borrow funds to accomplish some of their functions despite a lapse in appropriations. This category does not currently apply to DHS functions; however, Components should notify OGC if it is believed a function may qualify.

3. Implied by Law as Necessary to Continue Even without Funding

Pursuant to a determination by the DOJ Office of Legal Counsel, functions authorized by law to proceed during an appropriations lapse also include "those functions for which such authority arises by necessary implication." Presidentially Appointed and Senate Confirmed Officers and other political appointees who are not subject to the Annual and Sick Leave Act, 5 U.S.C. § 6301, 5 C.F.R. § 630.211, are exempt from a furlough during a lapse in appropriations. These appointees are entitled to compensation based on their status. This entitlement means that DHS is authorized by law to incur obligations for their pay. These appointees may perform normal duties during a lapse.

4. Necessary to the Discharge of the President's Constitutional Duties and Powers.

Employees who may be detailed to the Executive Office of the White House may be exempt.

Those who are engaged in the conduct of foreign relations essential to national security are exempt.

5. Necessary for Safety of Human Life or Protection of Property.

To qualify under the exception of protection of human life or property, there must be some reasonable likelihood that the safety of human life or protection of property would be compromised in some significant degree by the delay in the performance of the function in question. Specifically, the risk should be real, not hypothetical or speculative, and must be sufficiently imminent that delay is not permissible.

Any activity and/or function that qualifies for the protection of human life or property exception must be limited only to the extent that the Component Head determines that imminent danger to life or property would result from their termination or diminution. Administrative, research, or other support functions related to an exempt activity should also continue, but only to the extent that they are essential to maintain the effectiveness of those activities and/or functions that are engaged in the protection of life or property, and at a minimum level.

For example, law enforcement officers (LEOs) whose duties include protecting human life or protecting property are exempt. However, LEOs who perform administrative functions that do not directly and demonstrably contribute to such activities are not exempt unless their work is necessary to support activities that protect life or property. While law enforcement activities are exempt, the pivotal factor is the work being performed, not the law enforcement officer status of any particular employee.

EXAMPLES:

- Maintaining law enforcement operations, including drug and illegal alien interdiction
- Continuing passenger processing and cargo inspection functions at ports of entry
- Providing the protective functions of the U.S. Secret Service
- Maintaining counter-terrorism watches or intelligence gathering or dissemination in support of terrorist threat warnings
- Retaining minimal personnel to maintain telecommunications necessary for exempt activities

---

6. <u>Necessary for the Orderly Cessation of Functions.</u>

Agencies may obligate funds during periods of lapsed appropriations to bring about the orderly cessation of non-exempt activities, which OMB has determined should take no more than four hours. During that time, employee activities during this period must be wholly devoted to de-activating the function and upon completion, these employees would be released.

EXAMPLES:

- Performing payroll functions for the period just prior to the appropriation lapse
- Completing inventories of property and records to ensure protection of the Federal Government's interests and claims of affected private entities and individuals
- For "partially exempt" activities, the transferring of any ongoing work necessary to support an exempted function.
- Personnel functions to process furlough/reduction in force notices

---

The Appendix identifies total estimated exempt employees within each DHS Component.

C. Non-Exempt Functions

Non-exempt activities are all other activities that do not fall into any other categories. Employees in positions performing these functions should be furloughed during a lapse in appropriations. This could include employees who may have to be recalled at a later date, if the furlough continues for more than a week.

EXAMPLES:

- Planning (such as strategic, business, or budgetary activities)
- Research and development activities
- Most policy functions, administrative, as well as programmatic, unless those functions can be justified by the above exceptions
- Auditing
- Regulatory, legislative, public affairs, and intergovernmental affairs
- Training and development

D. Exempt vs. Essential Functions

Exempt functions are those which are exempted from work restrictions in the ADA and may continue to operate during an appropriations lapse. Exempt functions and activities are described in this guidance.

Essential functions are a limited set of mission-essential or mission-critical functions that must be performed to provide continuity of operations (COOP). Each DHS Component has identified and defined its mission-essential functions separately. The identification of essential activities is different than the determination of exempt activities.

Section IV provides additional guidance on the differences between exempt employees for the purpose of a lapse in appropriations and essential employees for the purpose of a COOP event.

E. Employees: Exempt vs. Non-Exempt

Exempt employees have been designated by their supervisors to perform functions or activities that are exempt from work restrictions specified in the ADA and may continue to operate during a lapse in appropriations. The term "exempt" employee only applies to emergency furloughs. Reference to an "exempt employee" for the purpose of government shutdown is not to be confused with an employee designated as an "exempt" employee under the Fair Labor Standards Act.

Non-exempt employees perform functions that are not exempt from a government closure. Non-exempt employees are subject to an "emergency" furlough and are not permitted to work. A non-exempt employee may be involved in the orderly closure of activities and functions. However, once it is determined that non-exempt employees have completed all tasks related to the orderly suspension of agency operations, the services of those employees can no longer be accepted in the absence of appropriations. Non-exempt employees may not voluntarily perform non-exempt services during an "emergency" furlough. Reference to a "non-exempt employee" for the purpose of government shutdown should not be confused with an employee designated as a "non-exempt" employee under the Fair Labor Standards Act.

F. Designating Exempt Employees

Components must designate in advance (before any potential furlough) those employees who must perform functions or activities that are exempt from work restrictions specified in the ADA and may continue to operate during a lapse in appropriations. DHS maintains standard notification templates, which may be used to notify employees that they are exempt from an emergency furlough.

The activities and funding of employees on detail to other Federal Government agencies and to Congressional offices must be reviewed as well to determine whether these detailed employees and activities will be designated exempt or non-exempt based on the function and the availability of funds. In making such a designation, the detailee's home agency supervisor should coordinate with the supervisor at the place of the detaileeship.

Exempt employees should only work on exempt activities during the furlough, including providing support to exempt functions and activities. With the exception of employees who are paid from other than annual appropriations that have not lapsed, exempt employees who work during a lapse in appropriations will not be paid. However, exempt employees will be paid when Congress passes and the President signs a new appropriation or Continuing Resolution.

Components should ensure that information on facilities, reporting officials, and systems available to employees working during a furlough is available and distributed to all of their exempt employees.

III. Procedures for an Orderly Closure

At the direction of the Secretary through the Deputy Secretary, USM is responsible for implementing the Department's general procedures for an orderly closure. The Head of each Component is responsible for ensuring that Component's compliance with the Department's procedures, and should not endeavor to make changes to such procedures without advance consultation with USM.

Given that the duration of an appropriations hiatus is inherently uncertain, the plan that follows describes Departmental procedures to be taken during the commencement and the first five days of a lapse.

USM, in coordination with the DHS General Counsel and Chief Financial Officer, will adjust the Department's procedures as necessary should the lapse continue beyond five calendar days. USM will also provide direction as necessary should external factors require changes to the Department's operations, such as may be caused by a natural disaster, catastrophe, or terrorist incident.

A. Implementation of an Emergency Furlough

1. <u>General Guidance</u>. Upon receipt of a notice from OMB through either the Office of the Secretary or USM that there is a lapse in fiscal year appropriations, Component Heads must notify their employees that an emergency shutdown furlough has been activated.

2. <u>Notices to Exempt Employees</u>. Components must notify their exempt employees that they must continue to work during an emergency furlough. The preferred notification process is by email. Notification also may be by telephone, by letter, or in person, if email is not feasible. Components may tailor this process to the degree needed to meet Component-specific requirements. Email messages to exempt employees do not require delivery receipt, read receipt, and return email.

3. <u>Report for Work</u>. Exempt employees must report for work during an emergency furlough. Any previously approved paid leave is canceled. An employee who refuses to report for work after being ordered to do so will be considered to be in an absence without leave status and may be subject to administrative or disciplinary action for not reporting for work. During a lapse in appropriations, all affected employees must be either (1) at work performing exempt activities (exempt employees) or (2) in a furlough status (non-exempt employees).

   If an employee is unable to report for work during a furlough and the supervisor or other management official approves the absence, the supervisor may change the status of the exempt employee to non-exempt and furlough the employee to allow the employee to be "absent" from work. When an employee is not working or performing exempt activities in compliance with the ADA, he or she must be furloughed and the furlough must be documented by a furlough notice. Employees should not be granted leave without pay for absences from work during a furlough. If legislation is later enacted to compensate employees who were furloughed, employees on leave without pay during the furlough would not be compensated.

Exempt employees who work during a lapse in appropriations will not be paid during the funding hiatus. However, exempt employees will be paid when Congress passes and the President signs a new appropriation or Continuing Resolution.

4. <u>Employee Leave</u>. Employees who are exempt from furlough by reason of being funded by other than annual appropriations may take paid leave (e.g., annual or sick leave) during a furlough. Employees who are exempt but not funded by other than annual appropriations may not take paid leave and must be furloughed during any period of absence. Supervisors must allow an exempt employee to continue to be absent from work for active military duty, although the employee may not use military leave or any other paid leave (e.g., annual or sick leave) during the furlough. Instead, the employee's status would be Absent-Uniformed Service (formerly Leave Without Pay-Uniformed Service).

5. <u>"Use or Lose" Annual Leave</u>. Many exempt (and non-exempt) employees may have accumulated annual leave that exceeds their applicable maximum annual leave ceiling. (Most employees are subject to the 30-day maximum annual leave ceiling. Members of the Senior Executive Service (SES) are subject to a 90-day maximum annual leave ceiling. Employees stationed overseas are subject to a 45-day annual leave ceiling.) Since exempt and non-exempt employees may not use annual leave during a furlough, any unused annual leave in excess of the employee's applicable leave ceiling at the end of the leave year (for instance, January 11, 2014 for Leave Year 2015) is subject to forfeiture.

Employees may request restoration of forfeited annual leave, if the annual leave was scheduled and approved in advance (see Component's internal procedures), later cancelled by the supervisor due to "exigencies of the public business," and the annual leave could not be rescheduled and used before the end of the leave year. A lapse in appropriations has previously been determined by OPM/OMB to be "an exigency of the public business," and employees' forfeited annual leave can be restored. (Also see the OPM fact sheet on "Annual Leave (General Information)" at http://www.opm.gov/oca/leave/HTML/ANNUAL.asp.)

6. <u>Weather-Related Leave</u>. Exempt employees are required to report for work on time even if, during a lapse in appropriations, OPM announces that "Federal agencies are operating under an unscheduled leave" policy because of emergency weather conditions. Although normally "essential employees" who are not designated as "exempt employees" should not come to work during a weather emergency occurring in the middle of a furlough, they should be aware that their non-exempt designation may change to exempt based on conditions and they would then be required to report for work. Should an exempt

employee be unable to report for work because of emergency conditions, he or she must be placed in a furlough status until such time as the employee is able to report for work.

B. Furlough of Non-Exempt Employees

1. <u>General Guidance</u>. The procedures outlined as follows apply to DHS operations that are non-exempt from work restrictions because of a lapse in fiscal year appropriations. They should be implemented by Component Heads upon receipt of a notice from OMB through either the Office of the Secretary or the USM.

   If a funding lapse begins at midnight on a Friday, furlough notices should be issued on Saturday to non-exempt employees whose next scheduled workday is on Saturday, on Sunday to non-exempt employees whose next scheduled workday is on Sunday, and on Monday for non-exempt employees whose next scheduled workday is on Monday.

2. <u>Employee Notices</u>. Components must be sure to contact all employees who have been designated as non-exempt including those on detail, on travel, in training/conferences, overseas, on leave, etc. Those employees should be provided advance notice of their non-exempt status. This can be accomplished verbally or with a "Notice to Non-Exempt Employees;" a template will be maintained and available through the Department's Office of the Chief Human Capital Officer (OCHCO). This notice informs employees of their non-exempt status in the event of a funding hiatus; it is not a furlough notice. Servicing Human Resources Offices shall immediately transmit the employee notices that supervisors and managers must distribute to their employees.

   Employee furlough notices must be delivered via email or in person using the template maintained by the Department's OCHCO. A read receipt or delivery receipt is preferred where feasible.

3. <u>Non-Exempt Employees on Travel</u>. Even with approved travel orders, non-mission critical travel should not commence within three business days of the date of a potential funding lapse. Non-exempt employees planning temporary duty assignments away from their normal duty stations at the time of a lapse in funding should change their travel plans and instead should report to their permanent duty station before the effective date of the funding lapse. Such employees should work with the Department travel management service provider to affect such changes and should be sure to terminate other reservations such as lodging or rental car.

   Non-exempt employees already serving on temporary duty assignments at the time of a lapse in funding may hold in place until their employing agency makes a determination that they must return to their permanent duty stations. Components should determine the reasonableness and practicality of changes to temporary duty travel on the basis of the length of the assignment and the time required for return travel, compared to the anticipated length of the lapse, and should in general minimize the burdens and costs associated with a return to permanent duty stations.

4. <u>Notice to Federal Employees About Unemployment Insurance, Standard Form 8</u>. It is possible that furloughed employees may become eligible for unemployment compensation and Components should provide them an SF-8 as the same time the furlough letter is issued. State unemployment compensation requirements differ; some states require a one-week waiting period before an individual qualifies for payments. Agencies or employees should submit questions to the appropriate state (or District of Columbia) office. (Also see the Department of Labor website "Unemployment Compensation for Federal Employees" at http://workforcesecurity.doleta.gov/unemploy/unemcomp.asp.)

   The SF-8 informs employees of their right to file a claim for Unemployment Compensation, explains the basic eligibility requirements, provides general information as to how, when, and where to file a claim, and describes the documents which the individual should take when filing a claim (20 CFR Part 609.20). Components must annotate the address and Agency Code of the separating federal agency where wage and separation information can be obtained. This document may be posted to an accessible automated information-sharing site used to communicate useful and required information that would normally be attached to the furlough notice.

5. <u>Shutdown Activities</u>. Non-exempt employees may be engaged in shutdown activities during the first four hours of the first working day of a lapse in appropriations, such as:

   a. Supervisor notifications to non-exempt employees that they are furloughed
   b. Consolidating and organizing employee notices, including email receipt/read notices and employee return emails, for forwarding to the servicing human resources office upon request
   c. Consolidating and storing files
   d. Safeguarding classified materials
   e. Protecting government property
   f. Notifying the public and other agencies of the shutdown of DHS operations
   g. Documenting the status of projects to facilitate resumption when regular operations are resumed
   h. Processing appropriate personnel/payroll actions and filing documentation

6. <u>Employee Pay.</u> Component human resource organizations should ensure all employees will receive compensation as regularly scheduled for time worked prior to the lapse. OCHCO will provide Component human resource officers with a special code for input into employee time and attendance systems (such as WebTA) to identify hours not worked because of furlough. Components must ensure such code is utilized to help prevent over-payment of compensation to non-exempt employees for time worked prior to the lapse.

   Non-exempt employees will receive pay for performing shutdown activities following enactment of an appropriations bill or a Continuing Resolution permitting such payments. Exempt employees whose salaries are funded by other than annual appropriations should continue to receive pay as regularly scheduled. Human resource organizations must also be prepared to respond in the event legislation is enacted during the lapse that permits some exempt employees such as military personnel to continue to receive pay.

7. <u>End of Furlough</u>. Furloughed employees will be instructed to monitor the media and to regularly check the DHS website as well as their DHS-issued electronic devices, such as BlackBerry or TREO, for notice on when the furlough has ended and when to return to work. (See Section H(b) for more information).

8. <u>Other Considerations.</u>

   a. Component Employee Assistance Programs (EAP) are expected to continue to operate during a lapse in appropriations. All employees – including those that are non-exempt, may benefit from counseling assistance from their Component EAPs during this stressful time. In addition, employees may want to contact their financial institution, credit union or learn about other options for financial assistance through the Thrift Savings Plan (www.tsp.gov).

   b. Any previously approved paid leave for employees in a component impacted by a lapse in appropriations is cancelled during a lapse in appropriations. In addition, employees may not be granted leave without pay during a lapse in appropriations. If legislation is later enacted to compensate employees who were furloughed as a result of a lapse in appropriations, employees on leave without pay during the furlough would not be compensated.

   c. Regardless of whether an approved Travel Authorization has been obtained, non-exempt employees may not start new travel in the event of a lapse in appropriations.

   d. In light of the uncertainty of the budget situation during a lapse of appropriations, Components should delay the enter-on-duty date for new employees and transfer employees (transferring from another government agency) who are scheduled to enter on duty on the first day or anytime during a furlough. Components should notify these employees that DHS is under an emergency furlough and they should NOT report for work until they receive further instructions. New and transfer employees should be in-processed after the furlough ends.

C. Management Controls

1. <u>General Guidance</u>. DHS internal control standards will continue for exempt operations during a temporary funding hiatus. Components with continuing operations must (if possible), modify or develop procedures to ensure adequate controls in a streamlined environment to achieve the same internal control results expected during normal operations. This includes ensuring adequate reviewing, authorizing, and approving

functions are in place. Additionally, Components must maintain key separation of duties for important business functions such as the following:

    a. Authorizations

    b. Records and documenting

    c. Custody of assets, whether directly or indirectly (e.g., receiving checks in mail)

2. <u>Record Keeping and Reporting</u>. Special care must be taken throughout the lapse in appropriations to maintain logs, formal records, and file copies of all transactions and expenditures to provide adequate accountability and justification for exempt activities, including the costs expended for exempt activities.

At the conclusion of the hiatus, Components must be able to achieve the same reporting outputs that occur in a normal environment. For example, at the conclusion of the hiatus, Components will process any backlog of accumulated transactions not entered into the financial system and report compliance with internal control standards. Examples of activities and documentation includes, but is not limited to, tracking obligation data, exercising contract authority, managing revenue collection activities, and processing exempted travel processing.

Component reporting procedures will include gathering performance metrics data during the hiatus period to capture costs and savings data at the conclusion of the hiatus. Components must have procedures in place such that when appropriations become available to continue Federal Government functions, Components can report all costs incurred due to the lapse in appropriations. See Section V, Reporting of Costs Incurred.

D. Financial Operations

1. <u>General Guidance</u>. In the event of a temporary funding hiatus, DHS and its Components will stop all financial operations and financial system operations, including processing payments, receipts or performing funds control, except for the following exempt activities:

    a. U.S. Customs and Border Protection revenue collections

    b. Federal Emergency Management Agency disaster payments

    c. Organizational Program Coordinators needed to support credit card programs for exempt activities

    d. Financial operations funded by U.S. Citizenship and Immigration Services fees

    e. Electronic travel approvals and processing to support exempt activities

Whether DHS will incur interest due to delays in making payments caused by the funding lapse does not provide a justification to make payments. Except for the activities noted above, DHS personnel may make a payment during a funding lapse only when the failure to make the payment would result in an imminent threat to life or property.

2. Accounting Center Operations. Accounting centers will not run funds availability checks during a hiatus. Therefore, Components must keep a clear accounting record so that the accounting center may process complete transactions into the financial systems when normal operations resume.

3. Documentation and Reporting. Ensuring proper documentation and internal controls when conducting financial operations during a funding hiatus is mandatory. Components must maintain and control documentation of all transactions initiated and processed during a temporary funding hiatus. When the hiatus is over, Components must be able to account for all activities and meet reporting requirements just as under normal operations. In addition, Components must collect performance and cost data which can be analyzed for the purposes of determining the impact of a hiatus. Components will provide specific instructions on what data to collect.

4. Travel Management. Minimum travel management support will be available to support exempt functions. Travel expense reports will not be processed during a lapse in funding, and reimbursements for travel costs will not be made until the lapse has ended. Each traveler with an individually billed account is still responsible for the timely payment of their travel card balance.

5. Bank Card Program. Purchase cards, travel cards, and fleet cards will still be available to fund exempt activities. Component Organization Program Coordinators (OPCs) will consider a reduction in spending limits for non-exempt cardholders to one dollar for the duration of the furlough. Each Component will provide support to cardholders for exempt activities through designated OPCs. Each Component will provide guidance and specific points of contact to its employees.

6. Reimbursements. Reimbursements cannot be processed for activities for which DHS Components receive reimbursements from other than annual appropriations if the servicing Component's activities are funded from a lapsed appropriation. Because the servicing Component's appropriation is lapsed, there is no account to reimburse until after a full year appropriation or a continuing resolution has been enacted.

E. Contracting

1. General Guidance. The "Department of Homeland Security Contracting Contingency Plan" shall be maintained and, prior to a lapse in appropriations, distributed to the Heads of the Contracting Activities (HCAs) with a list of frequently asked questions through an Acquisition Alert. HCAs must work with their Component Heads to proactively survey and identify contracts that, in whole or in part, support activities that will continue to support exempt functions. This will serve two major purposes for DHS contracting activities:

   a. To identify and maintain a list of contracts for which Stop Work Orders or Partial Terminations for the Convenience of the Government should be issued to contractors, and to allow Contracting Officers sufficient lead time to prepare modifications to de-scope contracts and prepare any necessary justifications and other supporting documentation for contracts that will be partially terminated.

    b. To allow HCAs to determine an effective distribution of warranted Contracting Officers to support an orderly shutdown and the management of contracts supporting exempted functions.

2. <u>No New Obligations</u>. DHS may not incur a new obligation by signing a new contract, by extending a contract, or by exercising an option when the funding source for that obligation is a lapsed appropriation unless the contract is required to support those functions defined as exempt for DHS, such as safeguarding human life or protecting property.

    a. The ADA prohibits agencies from incurring obligations that are in advance of, or that exceed, an appropriation. Thus, except in limited circumstances, DHS may not incur obligations when the funding source for the obligation would be an appropriation that has lapsed unless the obligation is needed to support those functions defined as exempt for DHS or is needed to address an emergency circumstance that immediately threatens the safety of human life or the protection of property. Even when a contract, order, agreement or other transaction may be awarded or modified in order to preserve life or safeguard property, DHS cannot pay the contractor until appropriations are enacted.

    b. In addition to those contracts directly supporting exempt functions, many contracts are fully funded. Contractors performing under a fully funded contract may continue to perform unless government oversight or day-to-day interaction with government non-exempt employees is critical to the contractor's continued performance during that period.

3. <u>Federal Employees Supporting Contracting Operations.</u> If there is a lapse in the appropriation that funds the federal employees who supervise or support the performance of a contract, those federal employees cannot continue these activities during the funding lapse unless the contract supports an exempted activity. Routine ongoing activities related to contract administration are not authorized to continue when there has been a lapse in the appropriation that funds the contract administration activities. In other words, during a funding lapse the performance by contracting officers, contracting officer technical representatives and contract administration personnel of routine oversight, inspection, accounting, administration, payment processing and other contracting activity would generally not continue.

    a. In the absence of federal oversight, DHS may however allow the contractor to continue performance during the lapse period if the continued oversight is not critical to the contractor's continued performance during that period. This is the case, for example, for all firm fixed price contracts and orders that are fully funded at inception. DHS does not have to issue an affirmative direction to the contractor to continue performance. Instead, the contractor continues to perform work in accordance with the contract. However, it is always prudent to communicate with the contractor to avoid potential misunderstandings.

b. Depending on the duration of a funding lapse, the absence of available federal employee oversight may lead DHS to reconsider whether the contract activity should continue to be performed. In particular, if the continued oversight during the lapse period is critical to the contractor's continued performance during that period then – where consistent with law and the terms of the contract – DHS should instruct the contractor to suspend performance.

c. Additionally, if continued performance is not statutorily required, then DHS should consider whether having the contracting activity continue is a sensible use of taxpayer funds in light of the lapse of appropriations. In this regard, there may be situations in which the continued performance of a contract would be wasteful due to the impact that the funding lapse is having on other agency activities.

For example, it may be wasteful to have a contractor perform regular trash collection every day in the offices of a federal building that has closed due to the funding lapse. Should the relevant Component head decide that continued performance would be wasteful and thus should be suspended during the funding lapse, appropriate contractual action should be taken (which would be part of the agency's orderly-shutdown activities). Contracting staff will need to work closely with Component procurement counsel in making and implementing these decisions to minimize costs to the Federal Government.

F. Grants and Other Forms of Financial Assistance

1. General Guidance. The "Department of Homeland Security Financial Assistance Contingency Plan" shall be maintained and, prior to a lapse in appropriations, distributed to the Heads of the Financial Assistance Activities with a list of frequently asked questions through a Grant Alert. Heads of the Financial Assistance Activities must work with their Component Heads to proactively survey and identify grants or other forms of financial assistance that, in whole or in part, funds activities that will continue to support exempt functions. This will serve two major purposes for DHS financial assistance activities:

a. To identify and maintain a list of grants and other forms of financial assistance for which Suspension or Partial Terminations for the Convenience of the Government should be issued to grantees/cooperators, and to allow Financial Assistance/Grant Officers sufficient lead time to prepare modifications to de-scope grants or other forms of financial assistance and prepare any necessary justifications and other supporting documentation for those projects that will be suspended or partially terminated.

16

b. To allow Heads of the Financial Assistance Activity to determine an effective distribution of Financial Assistance/Grant Officers to support an orderly shutdown and the management of grants and other forms of financial assistance supporting exempted functions.

2. <u>No New Obligations</u>. DHS may not incur a new obligation by signing a new grant or other form of financial assistance, by extending a grant or other form of financial assistance, or by exercising an option when the funding source for that obligation is a lapsed appropriation unless the obligation is required to support those functions defined as exempt for DHS, such as safeguarding human life or protecting property.

   a. The ADA prohibits agencies from incurring obligations that are in advance of, or that exceed, an appropriation. Except in limited circumstances, DHS may not incur obligations when the funding source for the obligation would be an appropriation that has lapsed unless the obligation is needed to support those functions defined as exempt for DHS or is needed to address an emergency circumstance that immediately threatens the safety of human life or the protection of property. Even when a grant or other form of financial assistance may be awarded or modified in order to preserve life or safeguard property, DHS cannot pay the awardee until appropriations are enacted that provide the necessary funding.

   b. In addition to those grants or other forms of financial assistance directly supporting exempt functions, some grants are fully funded. Those awardees may continue to perform unless government oversight or day to day interaction with government non-exempt employees is critical to the awardee's continued performance during that period.

3. <u>Federal Employees Supporting Financial Assistance Operations</u>. If there is a lapse in the appropriation that funds the federal employees who supervise or support the performance of a financial assistance program, those federal employees cannot continue these activities during the funding lapse, unless these grants or other forms of financial assistance are necessary to support an exempted activity. Routine ongoing activities, related to a grant or other form of financial assistance administration, are not authorized to continue when there has been a lapse in the appropriation that funds the award administration activities. In other words, during a funding lapse, the performance by financial assistance/grant officers, program officials, and financial assistance administration personnel of routine oversight, monitoring, accounting, administration, payment processing, and other financial assistance activity would generally not continue.

   a. In the absence of federal oversight, DHS may however allow the awardee to continue performance during the lapse period if the continued oversight is not critical to the awardee's continued performance during that period. This is the case, for example, for all financial assistance awards that are fully funded at inception. DHS does not have to issue an affirmative direction to the awardee to continue performance. Instead, the awardee continues to perform work in accordance with the grant or other form of financial assistance. However, it is always prudent to communicate with the awardee to avoid potential misunderstandings.

b. Depending on the duration of a funding lapse, the absence of available federal employee oversight may lead DHS to reconsider whether the financial assistance activity should continue to be performed. In particular, if the continued oversight, during the lapse period, is critical to the awardee's continued performance during that period, then – where consistent with law and the terms of the award – DHS should instruct the awardee to suspend performance.

c. Additionally, if continued performance is not statutorily required, then DHS should consider whether having the grant or other form of financial assistance move forward is a sensible use of taxpayer funds in light of the lapse of appropriations. In this regard, there might be situations in which the continued performance of a grant or other form of financial assistance would be wasteful due to the impact that the funding lapse is having on other agency activities.

Financial Assistance staff will need to work closely with Component general counsel in making and implementing these decisions to minimize costs and liability to the Federal Government.

G. Use of DHS Facilities

1. Generalꞏ Guidance. Procedures outlined below provide guidance on the management and disposition of DHS facilities and assets during a lapse in appropriations. They should be implemented by Component Heads upon receipt of orders from OMB through either the Office of the Secretary or USM.

   a. Component Heads shall notify the senior real property official to direct real property management personnel to oversee the temporary closure of non-exempt facilities, coordinate and support staff consolidation, and to supervise the establishment of designated facilities for use in support of exempt functions.

   b. A funding hiatus plan shall be implemented to provide notification and details for appropriate use of facilities. It should be distributed to the relevant workforces and should include the identification and contact information of real property Points of Contacts (POCs) for operations during and following a lapse in appropriations. The real property POCs should be designated staff who have the lead responsibility for facility shutdown and start-up operations.

2. Facilities Occupied with Exempt Functions.

    a. Consolidation – Consolidate exempt functions in the absolute minimum space needed to maintain exempt operations.

    b. Building Operations – Maintain minimum operations to support exempted functions.

    c. Security – Maintain physical security for exempted facilities including monitoring facilities as appropriate. The Headquarters (HQ) Office of the Chief Security Officer (OCSO) will maintain essential security support and services to DHS HQ's facilities and personnel, as well as appropriate and required service to DHS Components. Collateral and Sensitive Compartmented Information security support to HQs and Components through the Special Security Office Program and Sensitive Compartmented Information Facilities support will continue. This includes working closely with the Federal Protective Service to ensure HQ facilities and exempt personnel are protected.

    d. General Services Administration (GSA) Notice – Provide notification to GSA Building Management Representative of exempt activities that will continue normal operations in GSA controlled space.

3. Facilities Occupied with Non-Exempt Functions.

    a. Discontinue use – Ensure facilities are vacated. For DHS-owned facilities, ensure essential shutdown and start-up procedures have been defined for the impacted assets, and notifications given to service providers for major systems such as elevators, electrical, mechanical, water and sewer supply, and security.

    b. Building Operations – Reduce operating systems to minimal requirements needed to ensure asset protection and maintain safety measures. For DHS-owned facilities, utilities should be set to weekend settings, and building systems should be placed in sleep mode/weekend service levels-lowered to minimum levels needed to maintain life, safety and security systems. Confirm emergency back-up systems are operational.

    c. Security – Maintain physical security monitoring. The DHS OCSO will maintain essential security support and services to DHS HQ facilities and personnel as needed. Exempt facilities will be secured and card readers deactivated as needed. This includes working closely with the Federal Protective Service to ensure HQ facilities and exempt personnel are protected.

    d. Notifications – Provide notification to GSA Building Management Representative of vacated non-exempt facilities leased by GSA to DHS, and similarly to other lessors if applicable. For DHS-owned facilities, develop list of external notifications for use at time of a lapse in appropriations, such as monitoring companies, local safety and security offices, and mail operations.

4. <u>Mail Operations.</u> – Operational considerations for the Mail Surety exempt functions are based on assumptions that the primary mail delivery vendors, United Parcel Service (UPS), FedEx, and the United States Postal Service (USPS) will continue to process some level of mail for DHS and its Components.

   a. In the event of a lapse in appropriations, Components shall determine how to accommodate existing mail surety services for operational functions. Service levels and arrangements may vary from location to location but should utilize minimum staffing levels. Designated points of contacts shall be responsible for receiving items identified as registered, sensitive, medical-related, and items requiring refrigeration.

   b. Mail delivery: The DHS Consolidated Remote Delivery Site will deliver mail to the designated DHS exempt facility locations. The DHS Office of the Chief Readiness Support Officer (OCRSO) in coordination with the DHS OCHCO and the DHS OCSO will provide a list of exempt personnel during a lapse in appropriations.

5. <u>Transportation Shuttle Service Operations for Exempt Employees.</u>

   a. The DHS Shuttle service will continue operations and is available to DHS exempt employees utilizing the OCRSO HQ shuttle service activity.

   b. Shuttle Service support to U.S. Coast Guard, the Federal Emergency Management Agency and the Transportation Security Administration will operate at normal schedules due to limited access to public transportation.

   c. Limited shuttle services will be available for the DHS HQ components within the National Capital region (NCR) and the OCRSO will distribute guidance based on exempt functions at specific locations in the NCR.

H. Use of Mobile Assets and Personal Property

1. <u>Exempt Functions.</u> The guidance provided below regarding DHS Mobile Assets (Fleet, Air, and Marine) and Personal Property functions is intended to reaffirm the continuance of only those functions which are required for exempt activities. Component managers responsible for the control, maintenance, and operational readiness of critical assets necessary for the continuance of exempted activities must take the following actions:

   a. Determine the bare minimum number of support personnel necessary.
   b. Consolidate equipment, operations, and supporting facilities.

c. Ensure that only the minimum amount of recordkeeping necessary to document the expenditure of funds and disposition of assets.

d. Acquire only the minimum amount of parts and supplies necessary for continued operation of critical assets.

e. Secure all property not used for critical activities in a manner that protects the asset and ensures its immediate availability upon reactivation.

f. Discontinue all contractor support not directly associated with the maintenance of critical assets.

g. Discontinue the acquisition of new or replacement assets unless the new or replacement asset is critical to the execution of an "exempt" activity and cannot be sourced from idle assets within the immediate inventory or located within the organization's or Department's regional inventory.

h. Utilize shared mobile assets and personal property resources within the Component, Department, and where possible through inter-agency means.

2. Non-Exempt Functions. Maintenance and support activities and personnel whose absence would not cause an unacceptable interruption in the execution of exempted activities outlined by DHS HQ include:

a. Air, marine, and fleet assets used for training or administrative functions.

b. Operations and maintenance activities necessary to support training or administrative functions.

c. Home-to-Work Transportation not in direct support of exempted functions (emergency response on a 24×7 basis).

d. Department and Component management activities which do not directly support exempted activities.

e. Recurring inventory for the sole purpose of property accountability;

f. Record keeping including reporting (field level, Component, Component HQ, or DHS HQ).

g. Acquisition and procurement functions (excluding parts and supplies otherwise mentioned in this guidance).

h. Planning.

i. Work order management not associated with the continuance of maintenance activities associated with critical assets.

j. Oversight, audit, and assessment not essential to the mitigation of fraud, waste, and abuse during the lapse in appropriations.

I. Use of Information Technology (IT) Equipment

1. Exempt Functions. DHS exempt personnel performing exempt functions may continue to use their DHS-issued information technology resources including BlackBerry and other portable communication devices, computer software and hardware equipment without restrictions, except that some personnel may need to utilize temporary equipment at consolidated locations.

2. Non-Exempt Functions. Once OMB notifies DHS that a lapse in appropriations has commenced, non-exempt employees may use their DHS-issued electronic devices, such as BlackBerry, TREO, or mobi-key to receive furlough notices, acknowledge delivery receipt and read receipt of furlough notices, and acknowledge receipt of notices via return email.

   During a hiatus, non-exempt personnel may continue to retain and monitor their DHS-issued electronic devices for status updates and emergency notifications from their supervisors or other management officials; however, employees are prohibited from using this equipment for any other purposes (e.g., employees may only use their DHS electronic devices for one-way communication to monitor the status of the furlough, which is strictly an option (employees are not on standby duty). Failure to follow this policy may result in a violation of law, specifically the ADA, which has a criminal component, and may result in severe penalties.

3. Internet Services and DHS Network Access. The Department's public website will remain accessible, but will not be maintained or updated. The DHS network will remain accessible to support exempt functions.

J. Training Functions

1. New Hire Training. Under the guidelines of Section 124 of OMB Circular A-11, the training of newly hired employees, including those in law enforcement, is not an exempt function unless such training and related support activities are funded by other than annual appropriations. Upon a funding lapse, such training functions and associated facilities should proceed with an orderly closure.

2. Skills Training. Training necessary to maintain specific perishable skills associated with law enforcement functions is exempt. Such activities may include training of canine units, Federal Air Marshals marksmanship training, and Secret Service presidential protection exercises.

   General skills training, including such activities provided by the Federal Law Enforcement Training Centers, is not exempt unless funded by other than annual appropriations. Trainees who are on temporary duty assignment and receiving training at a DHS Component training facility may hold in place if a funding hiatus occurs and only extends for a short period of time (one to two days). Should the determination be made that a funding hiatus will continue for an extended period of time, the trainees should return to their permanent duty station, the planned training should be rescheduled, and the training facility should proceed with an orderly closure.

K. Travel Guidance

1. DHS personnel may travel during a funding lapse only when necessary for exempt activities, such as when necessary for safety of human life or protection of property as determined by DHS Component leaders in consultation with their chief counsel and chief financial officer (CFO). Any such travel conducted should be limited in duration and performed only when absolutely necessary with no alternative means of carrying out the exempt activity.

2. For travel funded by other than annual appropriations and not directly necessary for the safety of human life or protection of property, the presumption is DHS personnel will not travel during the funding hiatus. Exceptions can be made only with a compelling, written justification that specifies the direct connectivity of the planned travel to supporting one of the following:

   a. The safety of human life or protection of property.
   b. Litigation activities associated with imminent or ongoing legal action that cannot be delayed until the end of the funding hiatus.
   c. Other exempt functions.

   Prior to making reservations for such travel by operational Component personnel, the Component leader must provide the USM a signed certification, accompanied by the aforementioned justification, indicating that the planned travel and associated costs have been reviewed and approved in conjunction with the chief counsel and CFO within the Component.

   Prior to making reservations for such travel by DHS headquarters Component personnel, the Component head must provide to USM a signed certification that the travel is needed along with the aforementioned justification. USM shall coordinate review as appropriate with the DHS Offices of General Counsel and CFO, and make a recommendation of either approval or disapproval to the Deputy Secretary of the proposed travel.

3. International travel during a funding hiatus is strongly discouraged and requires written approval by the Office of the Secretary in advance of incurring any costs related to the travel.

IV. Procedures in the Event of an Incident Requiring Recall

A. Essential Employees.

An emergency situation may arise for which federal assistance is needed to supplement State and local efforts and capabilities to save human lives and to protect property and public health and safety, or to lessen or avert the threat of a catastrophe in any part of the United States. Such emergency situations may require certain DHS essential employees to report for work. Essential employees generally are employees in jobs that are vital to public health, safety, welfare, and national defense, front line law enforcement, or the operation of essential facilities and functions.

Although some employees identified as "essential" will likely be determined to be "exempt employees," many will not since they do not perform functions or activities that are "exempt" from work restrictions specified in the ADA – e.g., functions/activities that are necessary for the safety of human life or protection of property.

The categories of "essential personnel" within DHS are as follows:

1. Mission Critical Personnel. Those employees occupying positions and performing functions that must be maintained under all circumstances to ensure the safety and security of the Nation and its citizens. The critical nature of these positions is inherent in the position description (e.g., securing the Nation's borders, protecting the Nation's transportation system, etc.). These employees must report for duty regardless of the emergency or operating status. Employees whose work is critical to the ability of DHS to perform its national or homeland security mission.

2. COOP Personnel. Personnel occupying positions identified to sustain an organization's primary mission essential functions (PMEFs) and mission essential functions (MEFs). These personnel:

   a. May conduct these activities at an alternate site, virtually or through the observance of an alternate work schedule.
   b. Are expected to initiate and remain in contact with their Component during an emergency to maintain continuity of operations (COOP).
   c. Are Emergency Relocation Group (ERG) members and alternate ERG members.

3. Contingency/Incident Personnel. Employees who are in positions identified for possible activation, as needed, depending on the emergency, including:

   a. Personnel designated in positions that ensure three-deep backup to mission critical or emergency personnel.
   b. Subject Matter Experts (SMEs).
   c. Personnel in positions pre-identified as part of a Crisis Action Team, and other

operational teams established in response to a specific incident or situation.

    d. Federal Emergency Response Officials.

    e. Reconstitution Personnel in positions identified as Reconstitution Staff.

    f. Personnel in positions identified as Devolution Staff.

    g. Persons in positions identified in an order of succession.

4. <u>Emergency Personnel</u>. Employees who are assigned to positions required to sustain a facility or function in the event of a localized situation, such as inclement weather or a dismissal or closure of DHS operations or services. These employees will be expected to work even when DHS applies dismissal or closure procedures. Because of the diversity in Component missions, employee occupations/skills, nature of the emergency, geographic location, and other factors, the designation of emergency personnel will be the responsibility of the Component Heads. It is advised that Component Heads designate, in advance of an emergency, those personnel that provide operational support or perform support functions (including security and maintaining infrastructure) which must continue following the release/non-reporting requirements of other personnel.

5. <u>Exempt Employees</u>: Employees who have been designated by their supervisors to perform functions or activities that are exempt from work restrictions specified in the ADA and may continue to operate during a lapse in appropriations. See Section II of this Plan (*Procedures Relating to a Lapse in appropriations*) for definitions of DHS exempt functions and employees.

Management Directive 250-05, Designation of Essential and Exempt Personnel, and its associated instructions provide further guidance.

B. Recall of Non-Exempt Employee

During a furlough, a situation may arise under which an office or Component may need to recall a non-exempt employee to carry out an exempt function. Such situations could include (1) an unplanned or unexpected project or activity that qualifies as an exempt function; (2) a determination that existing exempt functions require additional personnel; or (3) a need to replace an exempt employee who is unable to work.

In such a situation, DHS may recall from furlough the minimum number of non-exempt employees required to effectively respond to a specific project. If recalled to work on a specific exempt project, such an employee may work only on that project.

Each Component must designate a Senior Executive Service employee, who is already designated as an exempt employee, to serve as its Recall Approval Official, and who will either approve or deny requests for temporary or permanent recall. The USM may consult with OGC as necessary and may veto any recall approval. The servicing human resources office should be informed. The procedures are as follows:

1. The Component must complete a Return to Work Notice, and have it signed by the Recall Approval Official. In particular, the form must include (a) the purpose for which the employee is to be recalled; and (b) how that function qualifies as an exempt function (e.g., how it is necessary to protect life or property from imminent threat). A copy is available from Component servicing human resources offices.

2. Prior to recall of one or more operating Component employee(s), the Component Recall Approval Official must provide to USM a signed certification, to be accompanied by the aforementioned Return to Work Notice, that the planned recall has been reviewed and approved in conjunction with the Component's Chief Counsel and CFO.

3. Prior to recall of one or more DHS HQ personnel, the head of that Office must provide to USM a signed certification that the recall is needed along with the aforementioned Return to Work Notice. USM shall serve as the Recall Approval Official for headquarters offices and shall coordinate review as appropriate with the DHS Offices of General Counsel and CFO, and make a determination of either approval or disapproval of the proposed recall.

4. Complete and send the Return to Work Notice by email to the employee. If the employee does not have a DHS electronic device (e.g., BlackBerry, TREO, or mobi-key access), the employee may be notified verbally by telephone and provided with the recall notice upon reporting to duty.

5. Once the project/function that the employee was recalled to support is completed, that employee must be re-furloughed for the duration of the lapse in appropriations. The employee must be issued a new furlough notice, with a new effective date.

6. The servicing human resources office will be provided a copy of the recall notice and any new furlough notice (along with all furlough notices).

C. Emergency Relocation Group

An employee may be designated both as an essential employee and as a member of the ERG. Essential employees must be ready, willing, and able to serve during emergency furloughs and continuity events without regard to declarations of unscheduled leave or government closures due to weather, protests, and acts of terrorism or lack of funding. Essential employees may be designated as exempt employees in such events. Designation as an essential employee requires that the Department Emergency Notification System, the COOP point of contact, and/or the supervisor is able to contact the employee for notification of emergency conditions applicable to the employee's designation.

An employee's manager or supervisor will advise him or her regarding what the employee must do should a continuity event occur during an emergency furlough. The employee should immediately provide all personal contact information to his or her supervisor, and provide any changes or updates in contact information as soon as known.

If an employee is on the ERG and his or her position is designated as non-exempt during an emergency furlough, the employee would not remain "on call" and would not be compensated for remaining "on call." However, in the event COOP is activated and ERG personnel are notified to report to duty, they would be compensated for the hours worked based on appropriate statutes and laws.

V. Procedures Following Conclusion of a Hiatus

A. Notification Procedures

Upon appropriate notification from OMB, the Secretary will notify DHS officials that the lapse in appropriations has concluded and order them to direct employees to return to work. The DHS Office of Public Affairs will ensure that appropriate employee communications are delivered promptly and efficiently.

Although employees likely will receive an email notifying them when Congress has reached a funding agreement, they will be encouraged to watch the news and regularly check the DHS website for additional information on when to return to work. Typically, employees will be required to return to work at the beginning of their next regular workday following the President signing a continuing resolution or appropriations providing funding for federal agencies.

B. Workforce Compensation

Without further specific direction or enactment by Congress, all exempt employees are entitled to receive payment for obligations incurred by their agencies for their performance of exempt work during the period of the appropriations lapse. This includes obligations incurred by non-exempt employees who performed shut-down activities. After appropriations are enacted, payroll centers will pay all exempt employees for time worked. NFC will issue additional guidance on payroll processing.

Depending on whether Congress enacts legislation to provide furloughed non-exempt employees with compensation during the period of furlough, OMB and OPM will issue additional guidance on employee compensation, benefits, and personnel processing.

C. Reporting of Costs Incurred

As soon as appropriations become available to continue Federal Government functions, Components must report all costs incurred due to the lapse in appropriations including, but not limited to the following:

1. Interest incurred for late payments.
2. Amount of discounts lost due to late payments.
3. Unplanned travel expenses to send staff home and to return them to the field.
4. Other costs of stopping then restarting operations, such as shutting down information technology systems.

VI. Appendix

U.S. Department of Homeland Security

Procedures Relating to a Lapse in Appropriations

Closure Times and Exempt Employees by Component

Office of the Secretary and Executive Management

I. Number of Employees On-Board Prior to a Lapse in Appropriations

As of December 31, 2014, the Office of the Secretary and Executive Management (OSEM) had 588 on-board employees.

II. Estimated Time to Complete an Orderly Cessation of Activities

OSEM expects to complete an orderly cessation of all other activities not identified as exempt functions within four business hours following notification of a lapse in appropriations.

III. Exempt Functions and Employees Retained During a Lapse in Appropriations

OSEM estimates 81 employees as the total number exempt and estimated to be retained during a lapse in appropriations. These employees are exempt since they are Presidential appointees, funded by other than annual appropriations, or necessary for the protection of life and property.

Office of the Under Secretary for Management

I. Number of Employees On-Board Prior to a Lapse in Appropriations

As of December 31, 2014, the Office of the Under Secretary for Management (OUSM) had 2,021 on-board employees. This total includes the Department's Management Directorate and Working Capital Fund employees.

II. Estimated Time to Complete an Orderly Cessation of Activities

OUSM expects to complete an orderly cessation of all other activities not identified as exempt functions within four business hours following notification of a lapse in appropriations, with the following exception:

The Office of the Chief Readiness Support Officer expects that it may be necessary to retain two employees for a period of an additional four business hours (totaling one business day) to accomplish the orderly closure of facilities and the government fleet of vehicle functions. These two employees will be necessary for closing down the functions of the government vehicle fleet and non-exempt government facilities. The additional time is required because of the necessity to close out the DHS vehicle fleet, which will involve the protection of government-owned property, and because the Department is geographically-dispersed with its facilities and assets spread over 40 locations across the National Capital Region. The intent is to close as many DHS facilities as possible and have exempt personnel consolidated at designated exempt facilities in the National Capital Region.

III. Exempt Functions and Employees Retained During a Lapse in Appropriations

OUSM estimates 239 employees as the total number exempt and estimated to be retained during a lapse in appropriations.

These employees are exempt since they are either Presidential appointees or necessary for the protection of life and property.

Analysis and Operations

II. Number of Employees On-Board Prior to a Lapse in Appropriations

As of December 31, 2014, the Department had a total of 794 on-board employees under the Analysis and Operations (A&O) account.

I. Estimated Time to Complete an Orderly Cessation of Activities

A&O expects to complete an orderly cessation of all other activities not identified as exempt functions within four business hours following notification of a lapse in appropriations.

III. Exempt Functions and Employees Retained During a Lapse in Appropriations

A&O estimates 381 employees as the total number exempt and estimated to be retained during a lapse in appropriations. These employees are exempt since they are either Presidential appointees or necessary for the protection of life and property.

Office of Inspector General

I. Number of Employees On-Board Prior to a Lapse in Appropriations

As of December 31, 2014, the Office of Inspector General (OIG) had 668 on-board employees.

II. Estimated Time to Complete an Orderly Cessation of Activities

OIG expects to complete an orderly cessation of all other activities not identified as exempt functions within four business hours following notification of a lapse in appropriations.

III. Exempt Functions and Employees Retained During a Lapse in Appropriations

OIG estimates 352 employees as the total number exempt and estimated to be retained during a lapse in appropriations. These employees are exempt since they are Presidential appointees, law enforcement officers, or necessary for the protection of life and property.

U.S. Customs and Border Protection

I. Number of Employees On-Board Prior to a Lapse in Appropriations

As of December 31, 2014, U.S. Customs and Border Protection had 59,546 on-board employees.

II. Estimated Time to Complete an Orderly Cessation of Activities

CBP expects to complete an orderly cessation of all other activities not identified as exempt functions within four business hours following notification of a lapse in appropriations, with the following exceptions:

- **Legal Counsel and Support**: Approximately three days are required to ensure the adequate transfer, resolution and/or disposition of pending procurement, contracting, budgetary, and personnel actions for the Office of Chief Counsel.

- **Labor and Employee Relations**: Approximately three days are required to close out labor and employee relations case files and other documents, and identify requirements of and render assistance to excepted legal counsel functions in matters such as active litigation in a variety of judicial and administrative venues.

- **Advanced Training Center (ATC)**: Approximately one day is required for ATC to facilitate the orderly relocation of approximately 150-300 law enforcement students that are locally housed. Because of the local housing arrangement, ATC requires additional time to execute an orderly cessation of its operations. This process requires coordination with local hotels, partner agencies (many of which are not within DHS), and contract employees, as well as the students themselves.

III. Exempt Functions and Employees Retained During a Lapse in Appropriations

CBP estimates 53,288 employees as the total number exempt and estimated to be retained during a lapse in appropriations. These employees are exempt since they are Presidential appointees, law enforcement officers, funded by other than annual appropriations, or necessary for the protection of life and property.

U.S. Immigration and Customs Enforcement

I. Number of Employees On-Board Prior to a Lapse in Appropriations

As of December 31, 2014, U.S. Immigration and Customs Enforcement (ICE) had 18,765 on-board employees.

II. Estimated Time to Complete an Orderly Cessation of Activities

ICE expects to complete an orderly cessation of all other activities not identified as exempt functions within four business hours following notification of a lapse in appropriations.

III. Exempt Functions and Employees Retained During a Lapse in Appropriations

ICE estimates 15,073 employees as the total number exempt and estimated to be retained during a lapse in appropriations. These employees are exempt since they are Presidential appointees, law enforcement officers, funded by other than annual appropriations, or necessary for the protection of life and property.

Transportation Security Administration

I. Number of Employees On-Board Prior to a Lapse in Appropriations

As of December 31, 2014, the Transportation Security Administration (TSA) had 55,791 on-board employees. This number does not include Law Enforcement Officers and other employees serving in the Federal Air Marshal Service (FAMS), the total number of which is Sensitive Security Information.

II. Estimated Time to Complete an Orderly Cessation of Activities

TSA expects to complete an orderly cessation of all other activities not identified as exempt functions within four business hours following notification of a lapse in appropriations.

III. Exempt Functions and Employees Retained During a Lapse in Appropriations

TSA estimates 52,604 employees as the total number exempt and estimated to be retained during a lapse in appropriations. This number does not include Law Enforcement Officers and other employees serving in the FAMS who are exempt; the total employee number of the FAMS is Sensitive Security Information not included in this document.

These employees are exempt since they are Presidential appointees, funded by other than annual appropriations, or necessary for the protection of life and property.

U.S. Coast Guard

I. Number of Employees On-Board Prior to a Lapse in Appropriations

As of December 31, 2014, the U.S. Coast Guard (USCG) had 48,261 on-board employees.

II. Estimated Time to Complete an Orderly Cessation of Activities

USCG expects to complete an orderly cessation of all other activities not identified as exempt functions within four business hours following notification of a lapse in appropriations.

III. Exempt Functions and Employees Retained During a Lapse in Appropriations

USCG estimates 42,147 employees as the total number exempt and estimated to be retained during a lapse in appropriations. Military members are exempt from furlough. Civilian employees are exempt if they are either funded by other than annual appropriations or necessary for the protection of life and property.

U.S. Secret Service

I. Number of Employees On-Board Prior to a Lapse in Appropriations

As of December 31, 2014, the U.S. Secret Service (USSS) had 6,336 on-board employees.

II. Estimated Time to Complete an Orderly Cessation of Activities

USSS expects to complete an orderly cessation of all other activities not identified as exempt functions within four business hours following notification of a lapse in appropriations.

III. Exempt Functions and Employees Retained During a Lapse in Appropriations

USSS estimates 5,818 employees as the total number exempt and estimated to be retained during a lapse in appropriations. These employees are exempt since they are Presidential appointees, law enforcement officers, or necessary for the protection of life and property.

National Protection and Programs Directorate

I. Number of Employees On-Board Prior to a Lapse in Appropriations

As of December 31, 2014, the National Protection and Programs Directorate (NPPD) had 3,064 on-board employees.

II. Estimated Time to Complete an Orderly Cessation of Activities

NPPD expects to complete an orderly cessation of all other activities not identified as exempt functions within four business hours following notification of a lapse in appropriations.

III. Exempt Functions and Employees Retained During a Lapse in Appropriations

NPPD estimates 1,748 employees as the total number exempt and estimated to be retained during a lapse in appropriations. These employees are exempt since they are Presidential appointees, law enforcement officers, funded by other than annual appropriations, or necessary for the protection of life and property.

Office of Health Affairs

I. Number of Employees On-Board Prior to a Lapse in Appropriations

As of December 31, 2014, the Office of Health Affairs (OHA) had 86 on-board employees.

II. Estimated Time to Complete an Orderly Cessation of Activities

OHA expects to complete an orderly cessation of all other activities not identified as exempt functions within four business hours following notification of a lapse in appropriations.

III. Exempt Functions and Employees Retained During a Lapse in Appropriations

OHA estimates 34 employees as the total number exempt and estimated to be retained during a lapse in appropriations. These employees are exempt since they are either Presidential appointees or necessary for the protection of life and property.

Federal Emergency Management Agency

I. Number of Employees On-Board Prior to a Lapse in Appropriations

As of December 31 2014, the Federal Emergency Management Agency (FEMA) had 14,024 on-board employees.

II. Estimated Time to Complete an Orderly Cessation of Activities

FEMA expects to complete an orderly cessation of all other activities not identified as exempt functions within four business hours following notification of a lapse in appropriations.

III. Exempt Functions and Employees Retained During a Lapse in Appropriations

FEMA estimates 9,684 employees as the total number exempt and estimated to be retained during a lapse in appropriations. These employees are exempt since they are Presidential appointees, funded by other than annual appropriations, or necessary for the protection of life and property.

U.S. Citizenship and Immigration Services

I. Number of Employees On-Board Prior to a Lapse in Appropriations

As of December 31, 2014, U.S. Citizenship and Immigration Services (USCIS) had 13,451 on-board employees.

II. Estimated Time to Complete an Orderly Cessation of Activities

USCIS expects to complete an orderly cessation of all other activities not identified as exempt functions within four business hours following notification of a lapse in appropriations.

III. Exempt Functions and Employees Retained During a Lapse in Appropriations

USCIS estimates 13,099 employees as the total number exempt and estimated to be retained during a lapse in appropriations. These employees are exempt since they are either Presidential appointees or funded by other than annual appropriations.

Federal Law Enforcement Training Center

I. Number of Employees On-Board Prior to a Lapse in Appropriations

As of December 31, 2014, the Federal Law Enforcement Training Center (FLETC) had 1,039 on-board employees.

II. Estimated Time to Complete an Orderly Cessation of Activities

Consistent with Federal Government-wide contingency plans, basic training of new employees in occupations that are generally designated as emergency will initially be suspended. Students and instructors will remain at the training site during the temporary suspension; if a determination is made after several days that the lapse in appropriations will be prolonged, the students and instructors may be given direction to return to their permanent duty stations.

III. Exempt Functions and Employees Retained During a Lapse in Appropriations

FLETC estimates 68 employees as the total number exempt and estimated to be retained during a lapse in appropriations. These employees are exempt since they are either funded by other than annual appropriations or necessary for the protection of life and property.

Science and Technology Directorate

I. Number of Employees On-Board Prior to a Lapse in Appropriations

As of December 31, 2014, the Science and Technology Directorate (S&T) had 462 on-board employees.

II. Estimated Time to Complete an Orderly Cessation of Activities

S&T expects to complete an orderly cessation of all other activities not identified as exempt functions within four business hours following notification of a lapse in appropriations.

III. Exempt Functions and Employees Retained During a Lapse in Appropriations

S&T estimates 26 employees as the total number exempt and estimated to be retained during a lapse in appropriations. These employees are either Presidential appointees or necessary for the protection of life and property.

Domestic Nuclear Detection Office

I. Number of Employees On-Board Prior to a Lapse in Appropriations

As of December 31, 2014, the Domestic Nuclear Detection Office (DNDO) had 121 on-board employees.

II. Estimated Time to Complete an Orderly Cessation of Activities

DNDO expects to complete an orderly cessation of all other activities not identified as exempt functions within four business hours following notification of a lapse in appropriations.

III. Exempt Functions and Employees Retained During a Lapse in Appropriations

DNDO estimates 7 employees as the total number exempt and estimated to be retained during a lapse in appropriations. These employees are either Presidential appointees or necessary for the protection of life and property.

VII. Total Employees: On-Board vs. Exempt

DHS Component	Total Employees On-Board, 12/31/2014	Total Exempt Employees
OSEM	588	81
USM	2,021	239
A&O	794	381
OIG	668	352
CBP	59,546	53,288
ICE	18,765	15,073
TSA[1]	55,791	52,604
USCG	48,261	42,147
USSS	6,336	5,818
NPPD	3,064	1,748
OHA	86	34
FEMA[2]	14,024	9,684
USCIS	13,451	13,099
FLETC	1,039	68
S&T	462	26
DNDO	121	7
TOTALS[12]	**225,017**	**194,649**

NOTES: On-Board employees include permanent and temporary employees as of 12/31/2014; the number of temporary employees changes on a frequent basis.
[1] The total number of employed Federal Air Marshals is Sensitive Security Information and consequently is not included in this table.
[2] Does not include personnel who work at Mt. Weather and other FEMA personnel carrying out sensitive programs.